A World of Difference

Following Christ beyond Your Cultural Walls

Thom Hopler

Study Guide

Prepared by Andrew T. Le Peau

InterVarsity Press
Downers Grove
Illinois 60515

InterVarsity Press is the book-publishing division of Inter-Varsity Christian Fellowship, a student movement active on campus at hundreds of universities, colleges and schools of nursing. For information about local and regional activities, write IVCF, 233 Langdon St., Madison, WI 53703.

Distributed in Canada through InterVarsity Press, 1875 Leslie St., Unit 10, Don Mills, Ontario M3B 2M5, Canada.

ISBN 0-87784-802-5

Printed in the United States of America

17	16	15	14	13	12	11	10	9	8	7	6	5	4	3	2	1
95	94	93	92	91	90	89	88	87	86	85	84	83	82	81		

Introduction and Instructions for the Leader

Let's face it. Fear is one of the main reasons we don't like to cross cultures—with Christ or without him. Whether it's a subtle grinding in your stomach or screaming rage, fear in its many forms holds us within our cultural walls. We are threatened by differences—not enriched by them.

Thom Hopler's *A World of Difference* can help us name those fears and thus begin to control them. A small-group setting can provide a supportive community for discussing and acting on this potentially uncomfortable material. The aim of this study guide is to help such a group understand Thom Hopler's ideas and to identify ways we should change in response to them.

There are eleven studies in this guide and an optional twelfth study for those particularly concerned to reach the campus. This makes it suitable for either a Sunday-morning class or a week-night series. Each study is structured in three parts. First, a *purpose* states the main aim of each discussion. The *discussion* section helps group members clarify what Hopler is saying, respond to his ideas and consider particular ways the book may apply to their situation. Finally, several *activities* are suggested.

The discussion section is designed to fit a 45- to 60-minute time slot, giving the leader an outline of questions to ask during each study. A lecture is not encouraged. The goal is to allow people to talk. The questions are designed to help you keep your group working steadily through the content of an entire chapter so that everyone will benefit from Hopler's ideas and have a chance to respond to his full presentation. It is expected that you will flesh out the discussion by using follow-up questions such as, "Why do you say that?" "Have any of the rest of you ever felt that way?" "Can you give an example?" or "What else does Hopler say on this point?" Also, give one-sentence summaries frequently to remind people of where they have been and where they are going.

Do everything you can to encourage balanced discussion. When someone who talks a lot finishes a statement, invite further comment by saying something like, "Does anyone want to add to that?" or "Does someone have another idea?" Doing this will encourage quieter people to make contributions. But don't be afraid of silences. If the group is working together, silences can be periods of creative effort. If a silence goes too long, rephrase your question. If someone is continually dominating or silent, talk with him or her privately about it. You will find other helpful principles for leading in James Nyquist's *Leading Bible Discussions* (IVP), especially chapter eight.

You may find the number of questions in the guide impossible to cover in the time you have. If this proves true, handle some by summarizing the portion of the text they cover and then proceed to the next question. Keep discussion brief for questions which ask you to evaluate Hopler's content, or use only the evaluation question that seems most likely to be of interest to your group. Decide beforehand which questions you can or will omit. At the same time emphasize that group members are free to challenge any idea Hopler sets forth. You don't want to beat people down with his conclusions.

As a discussion leader, you will need to take time (probably between two and three hours) to "make the study your own." Read the chapter(s) carefully. Write a brief answer to each question; then go back and, wherever necessary, put the questions into words and phrases you feel comfortable using. Make sure, however, you don't stray from a question's intent. All the questions are written so you can ask them directly to the group. Make notations on how much time you'd like to spend on each group of questions so you don't get bogged down. Finally, mark which questions you can skip, or summarize their answers if time starts running out.

The activities will take different amounts of time depending on the nature of each activity. Some offer ideas for further discussion; some involve further study or research by individuals or the group; some suggest outings for the group, like going to a concert.

Some activities can be undertaken as part of your normal discussion period while some will require a separate time together. This may mean (depending on which activities you choose) that you could have as many as twenty-four group meetings—twelve one-hour discussions and twelve activities also including discussion. But this number can be reduced by occasionally meeting for two hours—one for discussion and one for an activity.

We do not suggest that you do all the activities with each study. Select one or two that fit your group best. Involve the group as much as possible in the decision of which activity to select. Allow individuals to choose activities, if appropriate, and then report their findings to the group at the next meeting. Remember that discussion time for the activities is in addition to the 45 to 60 minutes suggested for the discussion section itself.

As the leader, you will want to evaluate the activities ahead of time—in fact, at least two studies ahead. Say, for example, that you are preparing to discuss chapter three. At that time you will not only want to review the activities for chapter three but for chapter four as well. In this way, if you wish, the group can assign individuals to do research ahead of time for chapter four and then make a presentation at the same time as your discussion of chapter four.

Also tell members to read the appropriate chapter(s) prior to each session. Encourage them to underline and ponder significant passages.

To summarize what has been said so far and add a little more, here are the ground rules to be explained to the group before beginning your first study: (1) This is a discussion. Everyone's contribution is valuable. (2) No one will be forced to comment though everyone is encouraged to. (3) No one's feelings are to be criticized. (4) People are free to disagree with what Hopler says. (5) Members should stay on the topic under discussion and the leader will bring the group back if it strays too far. (6) Everyone is expected to read the appropriate chapter or chapters before the session. (7) At the end of each discussion, we will decide as a group which activities we will do for that chapter or for the next chapter. We will decide who will do what, when and where. (8) The leader will attempt to begin and end on time.

Finally, as a leader, do not forget to pray for the people in your group throughout the week. And encourage them to pray for each other as well. The Holy Spirit is interested in working in our lives to bring them into conformity with the character of Christ. Prayer is one way of freeing the Spirit to work, and it reinforces our own openness to have him work in us. Prayer will bring you closer together even while you're apart. And, as Thom Hopler says, the unity we have despite our differences can be a mighty witness to the world.

1
"How Much Did You Pay for Your Wife?"

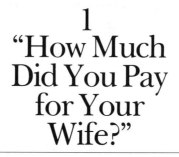

Chapter One

Purpose
To begin to understand how our culture affects us.

Discussion
1. To help us get to know each other better, let's each introduce ourselves, list the places we have each lived in for a year or more, and mention briefly what we each expect from studying *A World of Difference* together.
2. What four ways does Hopler mention to explain what culture is (pp. 12-15)?
Give an example of a mental roadmap in your life.
3. What are some values that give direction to your life? How do they guide you?
4. List some things that our society generally considers impossible.
Do you think these are also impossible in God's view?
5. How does Hopler illustrate that Western culture may not be more civilized than African culture (pp. 16-17)?
Do you know of any weddings like those Hopler describes? If so, what were they like and why were they that way?
6. How, on pages 17-18, does Hopler suggest the church has been affected by cultural blindness?
These issues will be discussed more fully in the coming chapters. But for now, what is your reaction? Do you agree or disagree with Hopler? Explain.
7. On pages 18-20, Hopler mentions some of the issues

and influences which have affected his thinking. What are some of these?

8. Summarize what you see to be the main purpose of this book.

Activities

1. List some of the heroes, important places and days, and key historical events for a subculture of which a group member is a part (church, college, company or the like). How is the importance of these shown in the subculture? Why are they important?

2. Go to a movie or play like *Fiddler on the Roof* or *Your Arm's Too Short to Box with God* and afterward discuss the differences in culture that it highlights.

3. As a group, attend an artistic event outside your culture (a concert, play, foreign film or art-gallery exhibition). Afterward discuss what you learned of that culture's mental roadmaps, system of values or limits of possibility.

2
Building the Family: Genesis

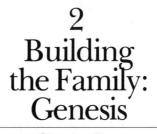

Chapter Two

Purpose
To understand how the teaching on families in Genesis interrelates with culture as a whole and our culture in particular.

Discussion
1. What do you most appreciate about the family you grew up in? Why?
2. Why, according to Hopler's view of Genesis 1—2, are we corporate beings (pp. 25-27)?
Does this mean that God did not create each of us as complete and whole people? Explain.
Do you think society tends to be more individualistic or more corporate? Explain.
3. In what four ways did sin break down relationships God had established (pp. 27-28)?
How did God begin to rebuild these relationships (pp. 28-29)?
What does this tell us about God?
4. How does the family of Cain contrast with the family of Seth (pp. 30-32)?
5. In Genesis 1—11, what were some of the ways God protected man from himself and kept him from self-destructing?
What are aspects of our culture that keep us from destroying ourselves and each other?

6. What five principles regarding the family does Hopler draw out of Genesis 12—50 (pp. 32-37)? Explain each in a sentence.

Which, if any, of these five principles were broken in your own family life? How has it affected your family?

Which of the five principles would you say is most needed in our society? Explain.

7. How, according to pages 38-39, should our witness in the world be affected by the teaching of Genesis on the family?

How can you apply this teaching in the next week?

8. How does the story of Beth illustrate the principle that God's time frame is not the same as ours (pp. 39-42)?

Do you agree that Beth should not have been encouraged to immediately stop living with Lou? Why or why not?

9. What specific situations are you involved with where our society's moral priorities may be at odds with God's priorities? (If you aren't involved in any, why is that so?)

What do you think your response should be?

Activities

1. Have someone or several research their roots, develop a family tree and then explain it to the group.

2. In groups of four, have each person share his or her family background using the following format:

(a) Describe your family (the community you grew up in, how the head of the household operates and so on).

(b) Describe your family economically. (Where does the money come from, where is it kept and what is it spent on?)

(c) What kind of work do your parents do (blue collar, white collar)?

(d) How are your parents seen or involved in the community?

(e) Where do you fit in the family?

(f) How aware is your family of the culture it is in?

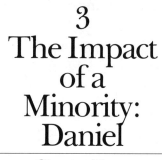

3
The Impact
of a
Minority:
Daniel

Chapter Three

Purpose
To see the impact a minority can have on the larger community.

Discussion
1. What minority groups are you a part of (in regard to race, religion, age, sex, economic class, politics, employment, ethnic origin and so on)?
As a member of such a minority, how is it difficult for you and your group to have an impact on the larger society?
2. After having been an influential people in Egypt, how did Israel end up as a suppressed people in Babylon (pp. 43-44)?
3. Why did Daniel and his friends stand above the best of Babylon (pp. 45-46)?
In what specific ways can obedience to God help us stand above society?
4. According to Daniel 3, how did the Jews end up with substantial influence in Babylonian society (pp. 46-49)?
5. What were the results of Nebuchadnezzar's finally turning to Yahweh (pp. 49-50)?
6. According to Daniel 5, why was Daniel able to maintain his power even though Babylon was overthrown by Persia (pp. 50-53)?
7. Read Jeremiah 29:4-7, found on pages 54-55. In what ways can you "seek the welfare" of the community in which

God has placed you?
How are you likely to meet opposition or persecution as you try to influence your society?
How will you cope with such opposition?
8. What can we learn from past and present Jewish and Black communities about influencing society at large as a minority group?

Activities

1. Read *Black Like Me* by John Griffin or *The Autobiography of Malcolm X* and discuss what it feels like to be a member of a rejected minority group.
2. Invite several members of an ethnic minority not already represented in your group to have a meal with you and to discuss how they relate to the larger culture.
3. Spend some in-depth time with a foreign student and listen to him or her talk about how he or she feels about being away from home.

4
The Center of History: Jesus Christ

Chapter Four

Purpose
To consider how the life and work of Christ can strengthen us to go beyond our cultural limitations.

Discussion
1. How did God work through each of the empires of Babylon, Persia, Greece and Rome to prepare the world for Christ (pp. 57-61)?
2. How has your culture been prepared for Christ?
What, therefore, are the most likely avenues through which the gospel can be spread?
In what specific ways could you work through one of these avenues to spread God's Word?
3. In what four relationships did Christ demonstrate a redeemed life (pp. 61-63)?
How did he demonstrate this kind of life in each case?
4. Which of these four relationships is in most need of reconciliation and healing *in your life*? Explain.
How can Christ's life help you in this area?
5. Which of these four relationships is in most need of reconciliation and healing *in society*? Explain.
How can you live your life to demonstrate redemption most effectively in the area of society's greatest need?
6. What limitations did Christ impose on himself when he became human (p. 64)?
What limitations do we have as humans?

What further limitations does our culture place on us?
7. How was Christ able to overcome his human limitations and resist the temptations of Satan (pp. 64-65)?
How does this offer hope to us?
8. Why, in Hopler's view, did Jesus emphasize building community more than evangelism (p. 66)?
Christ returned to the Father to send his Spirit. How does this affect your unity with other Christians? Be specific and practical.

Activities
1. Research the current state of the natural environment and formulate biblical principles for how society should relate to the environment. (Consider such topics as nuclear energy, abortion, dieting and overeating, family planning, waste disposal or use of energy.)
2. Consider the issue of self-acceptance. Have each person list what he or she likes and dislikes about himself or herself. How will these likes and dislikes affect your ability to relate to those in other cultures? (This activity is meant to spur discussion of how self-acceptance affects our relationships with those from other cultures. It should not be allowed to develop into a discussion of one another's weaknesses.)

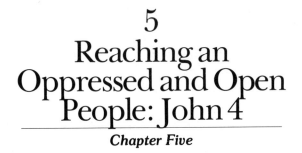

5
Reaching an Oppressed and Open People: John 4

Chapter Five

Purpose
To see that our contact with other cultural groups can and should be built on what we hold in common with them and on the truth God has already given them.

Discussion
1. What are some groups (racial, religious, social, economic) of people with whom you feel uncomfortable?

Why do you think you feel this way?

Why are differences in other people so threatening to us?

2. How did many Jews feel about Samaria (pp. 68-69)?

In John 4:4, how did Jesus show that his attitude was different from most other Jews?

3. What, according to John 4:5, is common in the heritage of Jews and Samaritans?

What do you have in common with one of the groups you mentioned earlier?

4. What are the two parallel story lines that run through John 4:7-27 (pp. 69-70)?

How did Jesus' reaction to the woman contrast with the disciples' probable reaction to the townspeople?

5. Hopler points out that the woman was possibly a prostitute (pp. 71-73). How do you respond to the idea of talking with prostitutes about the gospel?

How is Jesus able to set aside her social stigma and show that he is interested in and concerned for her as a person?

6. In John 4:19-24, Jesus de-emphasizes the Jews' theological differences with the Samaritans and emphasizes the basics they have in common (pp. 72-73). What secondary issues should you de-emphasize when speaking with those from a religious background different from yours? What primary issues should you keep in mind?

7. In crossing cultural boundaries, why can it be important to acknowledge honestly the faults, failings and weaknesses of your own culture, as well as its strengths (pp. 73-74)?

8. How do the two parallel story lines shift in John 4:28-38 (pp. 75-76)? Why does Jesus rebuke the disciples?

9. Why can we be confident that every group we go to with the gospel will already have some truth we can build on and learn from (pp. 76-78)? Think back to the group or groups of people you mentioned at the beginning with whom you feel uncomfortable. How can you find out what truth they already have?

Activities

1. At a social gathering of any kind, list all the cultural differences you see (language differences, taste preferences, fashion distinctives, economic diversities and so on).[1] Which made you uncomfortable? Why? (Allow 5 to 10 minutes for discussion for each person with a list. For example, allow 15-30 minutes for group discussion if three members made lists.)

2. Interview someone from a group with which you are uncomfortable (see question 1 above). Ask about his or her culture and try to discover as many similarities with yourself as possible. (Allow 5 or 10 minutes for discussion for each person who interviewed someone.)

3. Go to a foreign restaurant as a group and order from a menu in a language you do not know. Afterward, discuss how you felt about the experience.

[1]Adapted from Marvin K. Mayers, *Christianity Confronts Culture* (Grand Rapids, Mich.: Zondervan, 1974), pp. 28-29).

17

6
Dividing Power, Multiplying Disciples: Acts (Part One)

Chapter Six

Purposes
To see how the early church became and grew as a group of diverse people.

To identify ways our Christian community can be the same.

Discussion
1. Why is unity such a desirable goal for Christians?

How can this desire also be a source of division among Christians?

2. What were some of the differences between the Diaspora Jews and the Palestinian Jews (pp. 79-81)?

How then was the church able to get such a multicultural start at Pentecost (pp. 81-84)?

3. This multicultural beginning for the church soon drifted into a segregated situation. Why (pp. 84-85)?

How did the problem surface in Acts 6:1?

4. How did the apostles solve the problem (pp. 85-87)?

What results came of their action (pp. 87-89)?

5. What minorities are in your Christian community?

How could they be given independent power within your fellowship?

Do you believe they should be given such authority and responsibility? Why or why not?

6. Why were some of the Hellenistic Jews so upset with Stephen even though he gave a basically Hellenistic interpretation of the Scripture (pp. 89-91)?

7. In Acts 7:2-43, how did Stephen show that the Law had little to do with Palestine (pp. 91-95)?
How did he defend his position on the Temple in 7:44-50 (pp. 95-96)?
8. In what ways might our interpretation of the Bible be culturally limited? (If you don't know, how could you find out?)
How could a less limited view offer a broader base for unity with others?

Activities

1. Interview several people who are second-generation immigrants. Discover how they feel about their home country and how they feel about their adopted country.
2. Interview several first-, second- and third-generation immigrants regarding their feelings about their homeland and their adopted country. Discuss what patterns, if any, distinguish the attitudes of one generation from another.
3. Investigate services (both public and private) to recent immigrants in your community. (For example, is there bilingual education in the schools? Do government employees who deal with immigrants speak two or more languages? Do banks and utility companies have service representatives who speak appropriate foreign languages?)

7
Unified but Not Uniform: Acts (Part Two)

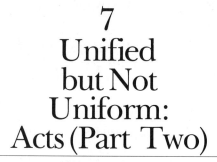

Chapter Seven

Purpose
To understand how God's people can and should be both diverse and united.

Discussion
1. How was Paul affected by Stephen and his message—both immediately and in the long run (pp. 99-101)?
2. The thinking of other apostles was not so profoundly affected as Paul's. How did the Holy Spirit overcome this barrier in Acts 10—11 (pp. 101-04)?
Why did the Spirit lead in such a step-by-step fashion?
3. The Palestinian Jews (and even the Judaizers in the church) said one had to be circumcised to be in a right relationship with God. What does your Christian fellowship say is necessary to be a Christian?
Would the requirement(s) automatically eliminate those in some groups (in certain denominations, for example)?
4. Are there certain actions a person could do which would automatically make it impossible for that person to be a Christian? If so, what are they?
Is there a broader definition of what it means to be a Christian that would be more in tune with Acts 10—11? What would it be?
5. Hopler notes that "the Hellenistic Jewish Christians from Jerusalem went into Greek areas but only spoke to other Hellenistic Jews about Jesus" (p. 105).

Have you noticed a similar tendency in yourself, to offer the gospel only to people whose culture you know well? Explain.

What will be necessary for you to be able to go to those in different settings or with different values?

6. How was Barnabas able to help reconcile the Jewish and Gentile Christians in Antioch (pp. 106-08)?

7. How does Acts 13 indicate that the Christians in Antioch achieved unity with diversity (pp. 109-10)?

Would a similar structure (integrated leadership representing several homogeneous subgroups) be valuable in your church or fellowship? Explain.

8. How was the debate at the Council of Jerusalem resolved (pp. 110-14)?

9. Why, according to Hopler (pp. 114-15), does the church need to fulfill both its "prophetic" role (going out into the world) and its "priestly" role (calling God's people to be faithful)?

To which side does your church or fellowship give the most emphasis?

How could the imbalance, if any, be corrected?

10. Looking over Hopler's conclusions on pages 116-18, what strikes you as being most crucial? Explain.

Activities

1. Each person can study a book of the Bible not highlighted in *A World of Difference* to learn what it says about culture and report his or her findings to the group. Some possibilities are Exodus, Judges, Jonah or any of the Gospels.

2. Discuss with missionaries the problems in separating one's culture from the presentation of the gospel.

3. Attend a church service outside your culture (perhaps Pentecostal, Roman Catholic or Black) and afterward discuss what your culture can learn from that expression of Christianity.

21

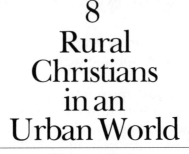

8
Rural Christians in an Urban World

Chapter Eight

Purpose
To understand how the church has and can use the overall trends in history to expand.

Discussion
1. What was the main thing you learned from part one, chapters two to seven, of *A World of Difference*? Why do you consider this so important?
2. Now look at Figure 1 on page 122. How did each wave threaten the church?
How was the church able to use each wave to expand?
3. Hopler says that the era of colonialism is ending and a new era of technology and urbanization is rising (pp. 125-28). Do you agree or disagree with this assessment? Explain.
4. How does a geographic frame of reference differ from a functional one (pp. 129-34)? Give examples.
5. Think of five or six people who are your best friends. What would you say is the primary reason you got to know each of these people and have remained so close? (For example: you went to school or church together; you played on the basketball team together; you are cousins; you work together or have similar jobs.)
6. What are other examples of how our society exhibits a functional frame of reference?
7. In what ways has Christianity tended to be geographic-

rather than function-oriented?

How has your fellowship group in particular been geographic- rather than function-oriented?

8. What would be the value, if any, of becoming more function-oriented for (a) the church at large and (b) your Christian group?

How could you become more function-oriented?

Activities

1. Survey ten people in the immediate geographical location you live in to discover how much they relate to one another and how much they relate to others outside the locale. Report your findings to the group.

2. Read Peter Wagner's *Our Kind of People*. Discuss the pros and cons of Wagner's proposal. Do you think his proposal is biblical? Why or why not?

9
Networks of
Communication

Chapter Nine

Purpose
To explore how networks of communication function and
how they can be influenced.

Discussion
1. Indicate which group within each of the following pairs
you believe has more influence—university administrators
or students and faculty; politicians or voters; pastors or
churchgoers; union leaders or union members; executives
of advertising firms or consumers.

Did you tend to pick those with formal authority or those
in the grassroots? Why?

2. On page 137 Hopler says, "Our rural mindset blinds us
to the importance of [human communication networks].
. . . Our orientation is toward impersonal power structures
and institutions. These are really what matter, aren't they?"
Do you agree that society in general places greater value on
the structures? Explain.

How does the article by Hitt illustrate Hopler's point?

3. How, according to Hopler, do we normally view the flow
of communication (and influence) within government (pp.
142-43)?

How does the example of the Newark public school (pp.
143-44) indicate that influence within the government does
not always flow from the top down?

What are some other examples you know of government
being influenced strongly from outside forces?

4. From your own experience or what Hopler says on

pages 144-47, how do professions seek to mold the values of their members?

Why is it so difficult to resist such influences?

How does Hopler suggest we influence these networks of communication for Christ (pp. 147-48)?

5. The third major communication network Hopler discusses is kinship. How much influence does your extended family have in your life? Explain.

On page 149 Hopler says, "I used a slogan during my four years of ministry in Newark: Every person is a doorway to a family, and every family is a gateway to a community." What is meant by this?

How might you use this strategy?

6. What are volunteer associations (pp. 153-54)? Why do people join them?

7. What volunteer associations do you belong to?

Which others could you or would you like to join?

How could you use these to expand Christ's influence?

Activities

1. Invite a professional to discuss his or her professional community using the eight characteristics identified by William Goode (p. 145). Try to discover how true these characteristics are of this person's profession.

2. Go to a local government agency with a problem to find out what would have to be done within the system to get the problem resolved.

3. View and discuss *Four Families,* a sixty-minute film available from New York University Film Library, 26 Washington Place, New York, NY 10003 for a $23 rental. (Give desired showdate and alternate dates. Also try to give street address not a box number.) The film compares patterns of family life in India, France, Japan and Canada.

4. Join a volunteer association. Report on the friendships you develop and on your opportunities for ministry.

10
Dynamic
Ethnicity

Chapter Ten

Purpose

To understand how ethnicity has affected us and how it should affect our witness.

Discussion

1. What is your ethnic make-up?

How do you feel about it?

How do you feel about jokes that make fun of your ethnic background?

2. How, according to Hopler, did the unbalanced melting pot develop in the United States (pp. 158-63)?

3. Look at Figure 5 (p. 164). Do you agree with the way Hopler has rated the level of influence the eight groups have had on the American value system? Why or why not? How, if at all, does Figure 5 illustrate your own experience?

4. The first two nonvolunteer immigrant groups Hopler mentions are Native Americans and Puerto Ricans (pp. 167-68). Why have their values generally been rejected by the American melting pot?

5. Why have Blacks found it difficult to assimilate to American culture (pp. 168-70)?

What is society's general attitude now toward Blacks (pp. 170-71)?

6. Consider the quote from *Time* on pages 171-72. Why do many Blacks oppose legalizing gambling?

What other factors does Hopler mention which indicate

that society's stance toward Blacks is a desire to control them rather than accommodate or help them?

7. What third alternative to government solutions and criminal solutions does Hopler propose (p. 174)?

8. Hopler says that three issues must be considered seriously to make this third alternative possible. Regarding the first, how do lines of communication in ethnicity affect our witness?

How should our witness be changed because of this (pp. 174-77)?

9. Regarding the second issue, how should ethnicity affect our view of missions (pp. 177-79)?

What specifically should you do?

10. Regarding the third issue, how should the dynamic ethnicity presented in chapter ten affect our attitude toward our own values (pp. 179-82)?

Activities

1. Visit an urban ministry in your area to discover how they are responding with the gospel to the city. (See your pastor for leads on who to contact.)

2. Read *Bury My Heart at Wounded Knee* by Dee Brown and report to the group.

3. Go to a local welfare office and go through the process of signing up for aid. What obstacles did you encounter? How long did you have to wait? Were you forced to miss work or classes? How did you feel?

4. Talk with a missionary about how his or her agency is facing the issue of appointing more minorities.

11
Christ beyond Culture

Chapters Eleven and Twelve

Purpose
To discover the basics of Christianity which can help us follow Christ beyond our cultural walls.

Discussion
1. Why is it important to have a firm grasp on the most basic biblical values before encountering another culture (pp. 185-86)?
2. Hopler says the two key values are truth and love (pp. 186-87). What two or three biblical values do you believe are most important? Why?
Why does Hopler believe truth and love are most basic (pp. 187-88)?
3. What problems can arise if we separate truth and love or emphasize one over the other (pp. 188-91)?
What benefits come from holding the two together?
4. What do we learn about truth and love from 1 John (pp. 191-94)?
When, according to Hopler's view of 1 John 4:1-3, should doctrinal differences interfere with our ability to have fellowship with others (pp. 194-95)?
What do you think of his analysis? How might you need to change your views and actions because of this?
5. Looking now at chapter twelve, how has the church in general been affected by impersonal, group-imposed standards (pp. 197-99)?

How has your fellowship in particular been affected?
6. Hopler suggests that the remedy for the bad effects of such standards is to look to Jesus as a guide for discipleship. How does Luke 9:22-27 connect Jesus' identity with the kind of disciples we should be (pp. 201-02)?

How are we trying to save what we have, to maintain our values and to conserve our culture rather than losing them for Christ's sake?
7. Hopler gives two examples on pages 203-05 of culture trying to bind us. What other limits does our culture impose that Christ would take us beyond?
8. What are the six signposts of discipleship (pp. 205-09)? Explain each briefly.

Which of these is most important for you as you seek to become a true disciple? Why?

Activity
1. Study Ephesians, Galatians or Romans 12—15, analyzing Paul's arguments for maintaining unity and handling differences among Christians.

Optional Study: Reaching the Campus

Appendix

Purpose
To help students and faculty understand how Hopler's model for ministry can be applied to their campus.

Discussion
1. How do residential and commuter campuses differ (pp. 211-12)?
What do you believe to be the most significant difference? Why?
2. How does Hopler's description apply to our campus?
3. What strategy is usually used to reach a residential campus?
Why is this strategy seldom effective with commuter schools?
[For those on a largely residential campus:] How has urbanization (that is, the development of communication along functional lines rather than geographical ones) affected even residential schools?
4. What suggestions does Hopler give for reaching commuter schools (pp. 213-15)?
Which ideas could we apply on our campus?
5. What else could we do to follow various groups of students back to their primary communities and build relationships there?
6. What suggestions does Hopler give to unify Christians in different cultural groups on campus?

How could we unify the Christians in different cultural groups on our campus?

Activities
1. Divide a page into five columns. In the first column list all the functional groups (freshmen, sophomores, graduates, international students, night-school students, ethnic groups, clubs, faculty, majors and so on) and all the geographic groups (dorms, apartments, city students, suburban students, fraternities and so on) on campus. In the second column indicate the numbers in each and in the third column the percentage each represents of the total school population. (This could require a fair amount of research. If so, assign different parts of the list to different people to investigate.) In the fourth column note the number in our Christian fellowship from each of the groups listed and in column five the percentage each represents of the total number in our group.

What groups are our fellowship most successful in reaching? Why is this so?

What groups are we least successful in reaching? Why? Write out a few specific steps to be taken in the next six months to begin to reach the three major groups our fellowship is missing most.

2. Read *The Impossible Community* (IVP) by Barbara Benjamin and discuss how the experiences of Brooklyn College might apply to your campus.

InterVarsity Cassettes by Thom Hopler

A CULTURAL SURVEY OF THE BIBLE series, 7200, 5 tapes listed
below
Building the Family: Genesis, *7201*
The Impact of a Minority: Daniel, *7202*
Dividing Power, Multiplying Disciples: Acts 1—11, *7203*
One in Christ in Truth and Love: A Biblical Value System, *7204*
True Discipleship: Luke 9, *7205*

All tapes $4.95 each.
Available from
InterVarsity Press
Box F
Downers Grove, Illinois 60515

Other books with study guides from InterVarsity Press
Basic Christianity
John R. W. Stott presents a clear statement of the fundamental content
of the Christian faith and urges non-Christians to consider the claims of
Christ. Paper, 142 pages. Study guide, paper, 12 studies.
How to Give Away Your Faith
Paul E. Little gives practical advice for realistic communication of the
gospel, both on and off campus. Inter-Varsity's classic book on evangel-
ism. Paper, 131 pages. Study guide, paper, 9-18 studies.
Joshua and the Flow of Biblical History
Francis A. Schaeffer expounds the book of Joshua and reveals the un-
changing realities of God's ways with people. Paper, 215 pages. Study
guide, paper, 12 studies.
Knowing God
J. I. Packer discloses the nature and character of God and how to get to
know him, not only informing the mind but warming the heart and
inspiring devotion. Paper and cloth, 256 pages. Study guide, paper, 22
studies.
Out of the Saltshaker
Rebecca Manley Pippert writes a basic guide to evangelism as a natural
way of life, emphasizing the pattern set by Jesus. Paper, 192 pages. Study
guide, paper, 12 studies.
Parents in Pain
John White gives comfort and counsel to parents whose children have
made life especially difficult for them and for themselves. Rather than
being advice on how to help rebellious children behave, this book deals
with the feelings of failure many parents share. Paper, 245 pages. Study
guide, paper, 12 studies.